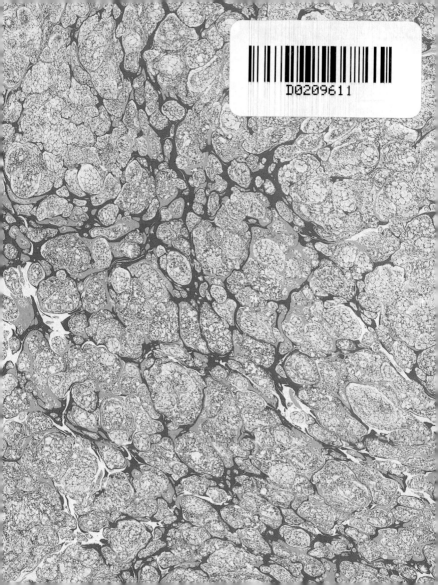

THE BANTAM LIBRARY
of Culinary Arts™

Oils, Vinegars &
SEASONINGS

JILL NORMAN

BANTAM BOOKS

NEW YORK · TORONTO · LONDON · SYDNEY · AUCKLAND

A DORLING KINDERSLEY BOOK

OILS, VINEGARS & SEASONINGS

A BANTAM BOOK/PUBLISHED BY ARRANGEMENT WITH
DORLING KINDERSLEY LIMITED

PRINTING HISTORY
DORLING KINDERSLEY EDITION
PUBLISHED IN GREAT BRITAIN IN 1992

BANTAM EDITION/MAY 1992

EDITOR   MARK RONAN
SENIOR EDITOR   CAROLYN RYDEN
AMERICAN EDITOR   BECKY CABAZA
DESIGN   MATHEWSON BULL
PHOTOGRAPHER   DAVE KING

Every effort has been made to provide accurate conversions from metric to American measures,
though some ingredient amounts have been rounded off to the closest American measure.

LIBRARY OF CONGRESS CATALOGING-IN-PUBLICATION DATA
NORMAN, JILL.
OILS, VINEGARS & SEASONINGS/JILL NORMAN.
P. CM. — (THE BANTAM LIBRARY OF CULINARY ARTS)
INCLUDES INDEX.
ISBN 0–553–08523–9
1. CONDIMENTS. I. TITLE. II. TITLE: OILS, VINEGARS, AND
SEASONINGS. III. SERIES.
TX819.A1N67 1992
641.6'382–DC20
91–36289 CIP

PRINTED AND BOUND IN HONG KONG BY IMAGO
0 9 8 7 6 5 4 3 2 1

C O N T E N T S

INTRODUCTION

*W*ITHOUT SEASONING, *our food would be very dull indeed. In his* Grand Dictionnaire de Cuisine, *1873, Dumas does not define the word, but instead recounts the story of the chevalier d'Albignac who made his fortune in London by seasoning salads. Following a request from fellow diners in a tavern to prepare a salad in the French manner, d'Albignac became sought-after in private houses, rushing from one to the other with his box of flavored vinegars and oils, soy sauce, caviar, truffles, anchovies, ketchups, gravy and even egg yolks for mayonnaise. He eventually marketed similar boxes and retired to France a rich man.*

Seasoning is "something added to a dish which gives it a distinctive or appetizing flavor," says the Oxford English Dictionary. *The adding is done during preparation, whereas relishes or condiments are added at table. Seasoning is about blending complementary flavors so that no one overpowers the others. Seasonings can be classified by their predominant taste: salt, sour, bitter, sweet, pungent.*

Salt is our most distinctive seasoning; without it food tastes insipid. It is an essential part of our diet, yet it should be eaten only in small amounts. Saltiness crops up in other seasonings – anchovy paste, soy preparations, fish sauce – because salt is used as a preservative. The sour, occasionally bitter taste is found in vinegars, and in essences and sauces with an acid base. Italian fruit mustards combine sweet and sour with a hint of the pungent, and clear pungency comes from mustard, pepper, and, of course, chilies.

The most elementary seasonings in a Western kitchen are likely to include salt, pepper, mustard, vinegar and oil, supported by at least a few herbs and spices. The staples of the oriental cook are soy, oil, salt and chilies, with the essential addition of fish sauce in Southeast Asia, and of some spices and herbs. From India to the Middle East salt and oil dominate, supported heavily by spices and herbs and the acid flavors of vinegar and lemon juice.

Many of the seasonings of the Far East are still new in the West; their pungent aroma may be disconcerting initially, but it mellows during

Tabasco sauce advertisement

cooking and in combination with other foods. Dried fish, trassi and fish sauce, used in small amounts, gave richness and delicacy to the foods of Thailand, Malaysia and Indonesia. Sambals and ketjaps from Indonesia are worth exploring and comparing with Chinese and Japanese chili and soy preparations.

This little book is intended as an introduction to familiar and less well-known seasonings; to encourage sampling a different oil or a flavored vinegar, or using with confidence the flavorings of different cultures.

OILS FOR FLAVORING

*O*IL USED IN COOKING *and for flavoring has little flavor in itself, but some oils contain traces of other substances which give them flavor. In some traditional oils a fine flavor is created; for the cook these cold-pressed oils which retain clear indications of their origin are the best. Different regions produce oils from different plants and each has its own characteristics. Olive oil is the most important oil of the Mediterranean region. Green olives are crushed and pressed gently to squeeze the oil from the olive mass. The first-pressed extra virgin oil is the best; it has a deep color and its acid content is less than 1 percent. The next three grades of virgin oil have higher acidity. More basic oils are made from the second-pressed oil and residue which is refined. The better the quality, the more intense the olive flavor. Extra virgin oil is perfect for salads, pasta and sauces; a lighter oil may be preferred for cooking.*

Oils are expressed from many nuts; hazelnut and walnut are most used in the home kitchen. They taste strongly of their origins and are best with bitter greens, potato and vegetable salads. The flavor diminishes when they are heated. Nut oils go rancid, so buy small quantities.

Extra virgin olive oil

Sesame oil from China and Japan has a deep amber color and nutty aroma. It is pressed from toasted seeds, which means that it burns easily when heated. A spoonful is added at the end of cooking to give flavor to soups and stir-fries. It is excellent in dressings for cold vegetable dishes. In southern India and the Middle East sesame oil extracted from raw seeds is widely used for all forms of cooking.

Olive oil   *Walnut oil*   *Hazelnut oil*   *Sesame oil*

OILS FOR COOKING

*O*ILS THAT *are high in mono-unsaturated and polyunsaturated fatty acids are beneficial in reducing cholesterol levels and the incidence of heart disease. Olive oil, followed by peanut oil, is the main mono-unsaturated oil; safflower, soybean and sunflower are highest in polyunsaturates, and coconut the highest by far in saturated fats. Italian research shows that extra virgin olive oil is easily digested, then come sunflower, peanut, sesame and corn oils. Sunflower seeds contain as much as 40 percent pale yellow oil, which is widely used throughout the Western world. It is virtually tasteless and blends well with the other oils. It can be a useful light oil for salad dressings and preparing mayonnaise.*

Corn oil is extracted from the germ of corn. It is easy to identify by its deep gold color. High in polyunsaturates and fairly high in mono-unsaturates, it is a popular, inexpensive "healthy" oil, best used for frying. Its flavor is rather crude when used in its natural state. Corn oil is used extensively for making margarine and in commercial baking.

Sunflower oil

Rapeseed, or colza oil, is processed worldwide; every journey in spring reveals fields of yellow rape. The oil is bland, heats well and is much used in Indian cooking. Grapeseed oil is a by-product of winemaking in southern France. Its color can be quite greenish, it has a delicate flavor and is good for dressings. It does not burn easily when heated. Mustard oil is the main cooking oil in northern India; it is rarely used uncooked. The mustard aroma decreases on heating.

Corn oil   *Rapeseed oil*   *Grapeseed oil*   *Mustard oil*

WINE & CIDER VINEGARS

*T*HE WORD VINEGAR *comes from the French* vin aigre *meaning sour wine. Vinegar has been used for as long as wine has been made, for its development is an entirely natural process. If an alcoholic liquid with less than about 18 percent alcohol is exposed to air, bacteria will attack the alcohol and turn it into acetic acid; this sour liquid is vinegar. Acetic acid has some flavors as well as sourness, but the taste of a vinegar comes from volatile compounds present in the original wine, which give it fruity or aromatic tones. The better the wine, the better the vinegar. Good vinegar is made slowly in barrels by traditional methods; newer processes use huge tanks and quick fermentation at high temperatures which drives off volatile flavors.*

Wine vinegar is produced in all regions where wine is made, from red or white wine, and from fortified wine like sherry. Sherry vinegar may be made from sherry or from unfermented grape must. The new vinegar goes into maturing vats and may then become vinegar of a single year, or goes into a solera system (see p. 12) just as sherry does, which permits it to be blended over several years. The bottled vinegar may be blends of single years, soleras or both. Its pungent flavor retains the taste of sherry.

Red wine vinegar

Cider vinegar, from cider or specially fermented apple juice, is low in acetic acid and can retain an apple taste. Cider and honey vinegar has a fine flavor.

Vinegars flavored with herbs, spices, fruits and flowers are easy to make; simply infuse the flavoring in a bottle of vinegar for some days.

White wine vinegar

Sherry vinegar

Cider vinegar

Wine vinegar with herbes de Provence

OTHER VINEGARS

$\mathcal{B}$ALSAMIC VINEGAR *is a fine, aged vinegar from Modena in Italy. The must from Trebbiano grapes is boiled slowly to sterilize it and concentrate the sugar. It goes into large barrels with some vinegar and a vinegar mother (a cultivated starter), and ferments for several years.*

The vinegar is matured in a system similar to a sherry solera: a proportion of the young vinegar is drawn off into a cask of older vinegar, and so on through a system of progressively smaller barrels. The vinegar to be used is drawn from the smallest cask. The casks are made from different woods – oak, chestnut, cherry, mulberry, ash – and each one imparts flavor to the vinegar. Balsamic vinegar may be 10 years old or up to 100. It is deep in color with a syrupy consistency, and a complex, full, sweet-sour taste. Use sparingly; it has a pronounced character.

Malt vinegar   *Balsamic vinegar*

Never cook with it but add to food just as it is served to enhance the flavors.

Rice vinegar *Chinese black vinegar*

Vinegars from non-wine-producing areas are made from grain and other fruits. Malt vinegar is essentially beer vinegar, made from grain and malt, but without the hops. It may be colored with caramel. It has few aromatic flavors and can be harsh. Rice vinegar is produced in China and Japan. The color varies from pale gold to colorless, and the sourness tends to be milder than Western vinegars. Chinese vinegars have a sharp, refreshing taste; Japanese vinegars are sweeter and can be weak. Rice vinegar can be used for all kinds of cooking. Chinese black vinegar may be made from wheat, millet or sorghum instead of rice. The best is aged for several years like balsamic vinegar. Good black vinegar has a strong, pleasantly bitter and smoky flavor. Include it in dressings for stir-fried or steamed vegetables with sugar, salt, oil and wine. Unlike balsamic vinegar, it does not suffer from brief heating.

SALT

"*THIS MINERAL is like unto the four elements – earth, air, fire and water. So universal, so necessary to life, it is the fifth element.*" Jean de Marcounille, 1584. Salt, sodium chloride, is one of the basic tastes detected by the palate, and it is probably the most widely used flavoring. Food without salt can be dull, but we now know to use it in moderation. The body only needs supplementary salt when perspiring profusely.

Salt may be evaporated from sea water; the traditional way was to heat the water in wide pans until the salt crystallized. Rock salt, found in deposits from prehistoric seas, may be mined, but it is now more usual to pump water into the salt deposit, and then evaporate the brine.

Rock salt

Round sea salt crystals

Flaked sea salt crystals

Sea and rock salt should have no additives, but ordinary table salt contains magnesium carbonate. Pure salt has a more concentrated flavor and brings out other flavors in food.

Indian black salt

Table salt

Always use pure salt, whether large crystals or finely ground, for preserving food. The flavor and saltiness of salt vary because of trace elements. Indian black salt is aromatic and smoky rather than salty; it is used in combination with spices. Spiced salts are popular in many regions. The Japanese blend sesame and salt, the Chinese, pepper and salt, and European "kitchen pepper," a blend of salt and assorted spices, was common in the 19th century.

PEPPER

THE MOST IMPORTANT *spice in the West*, Piper nigrum *is a tropical vine native to India's Malabar coast. Black, white and green peppercorns come from the same plant. Maturing green fruits are picked, fermented and dried in the sun to produce black peppercorns.*

Mixed peppercorns

Ground black pepper

The white peppercorns are made from ripe, reddening berries soaked in water and the skins taken off before drying. Green ones are immature fruits, preserved in brine or by freeze-drying. Pepper has a pungent, woody aroma; black is less biting than white; green has a clean, milder taste. Use whole in stocks and pickles; crushed for spice mixtures and marinades; freshly ground for finished dishes and at table.

MUSTARD

*M*USTARDS BELONG TO *the* Brassica *family and are grown widely throughout the temperate world.* B. hirta, *white mustard, is mildly hot and much used in North America; brown mustard,* B. juncea, *is the commercial crop which has taken over from black mustard,* B. nigra. *Hot and aromatic, brown mustard is much used in Indian cooking and for Dijon mustard.*

Smooth mustard

Whole grain mustard

Italian fruit mustard

Pear

Smooth mustard is made by grinding the seeds and mixing with water, vinegar, wine, salt, spices or herbs. Whole grain mustard is usually a blend of white and brown seeds with other flavorings. The Italian fruit preserve, *mostarda di Cremona,* is a mild accompaniment to cold meats. Fruits such as cherries, pears, apples, figs and pumpkin are cooked in syrup; the syrup is reduced and flavored with mustard.

Fig

Pumpkin

PASTES & SAUCES

A WELL SELECTED STOCK *of these will always prove a convenient resource in simple cookery for giving colour and flavour to soups, gravies and made dishes," said Eliza Acton* in Modern Cookery, 1845. *Store sauces, as essences and ketchups were called in the 19th century, were based on soy, vinegar, garlic, chilies, horseradish and spices. The other common ingredients were walnuts, mushrooms, tomatoes, lemons, anchovies and onions.*

Chili

Garlic

Ginger

Anchovy paste

Worcestershire sauce "prepared in Worcester since 1837 to the unique secret recipe" originated when a barrel of spiced vinegar made to an Indian recipe was forgotten in the cellar of Messrs. Lea and Perrins. It includes chili, garlic and ginger.

Worcestershire sauce

Small amounts of salted anchovies pounded with other ingredients give a subtle depth of flavor that is not easy to place. *Tapenade, bagna cauda*, anchovy paste and anchovy butter have a more pronounced anchovy taste.

Mushroom ketchup made with salt, spices, vinegar and soy is a useful addition to winter stews.

A primary ingredient of oriental cooking, soy sauce is fermented from soy bean meal and wheat, then aged. Dark soy is aged longer than light and has added molasses. Use light with fish and vegetables, dark with red meats. Japanese soy sauce is called *shoyu*.

Mushroom ketchup

Light soy sauce

Dark soy sauce

SOY-BASED PASTES

*D*OZENS OF SOY PRODUCTS *are made in Asia; protein-rich* miso *is a Japanese staple, eaten virtually every day, most often as* miso *soup. Fermented and aged in a similar way to soy sauce,* miso *may be light, dark, smooth or coarse. Red* miso *is sweet or savory, good for winter soups; yellow is salty and tart, good for dips, dressings and grills.*

Yellow miso

The best bean paste, which comes from Szechuan and Hunan, contains whole beans; there is also a smooth version. Bean paste, often flavored with chilies or garlic, is essential to the cooking of north-western China.

Hoisin sauce comes from Canton; it is jam-like or runny, sweetly garlicky and spicy, excellent spread on meat to be grilled.

Red miso

Fermented black beans Salted, fermented black beans are a popular Chinese seasoning. Their winey flavor goes well with fish and vegetables, particularly combined with ginger, garlic and dry sherry. They keep indefinitely. Indonesian *ketjap* is a thick, heavy soy sauce; two sorts are common: *ketjap manis*, flavored with palm syrup, star anise and galangal; *ketjap asijn*, lighter and less sweet.

Bean paste

Ketjap manis

Hoisin

FISH SAUCES

Fermented fish sauces, liquamen and garum were prized by Roman gourmets. Today, these strong-smelling sauces are more common in Southeast Asian food. Fish, often anchovies, are packed in brine and fermented in the sun for several months. The drained liquid, called nam pla *in Thailand,* nuoc mam *in Vietnam, is used in many dishes or as a dip. The salty taste is milder than the smell.*

Dried and ground shrimps are used as a flavoring: a good addition to pumpkin soup. Anchovy, or thick fish sauce is a blend of ground anchovies and fish sauce. Less pungent than clear fish sauce, it combines well with coconut cream.

Small dried shrimps

Clear fish sauce

Large dried shrimps

Anchovy sauce

Trassi in Indonesia, *blachan* in Malaysia,
this brown paste of rotted shrimps
smells strongly of meat extract. It is
always fried or dry-roasted (best
done wrapped in foil) before
use. An essential ingredient
throughout Southeast Asia,
its flavor is complex and milder
than its smell. Oyster sauce
varies greatly in quality. A
Cantonese staple, it was originally
made with oysters, water and salt, but
many versions are now full of caramel,
monosodium glutamate, sugar
and starch. Useful
for seasoning noodles
and vegetables.

Trassi

Oyster sauce

CHILI SAUCES

*C*HILIES CROP UP *in cooking in all parts of the world, fresh or dried, in pastes and sauces and oils. Chili oil is made by infusing chilies in vegetable or sesame oil. A few drops can be added to a dressing or a dipping sauce for meats and vegetables. Tabasco is a pure, fiery sauce made with chilies, vinegar and salt. West Indian hot pepper sauces often include onions and spices. Chinese versions have tamarind, Szechuan pepper, star anise, and sometimes sugar.*

Chinese chili pastes often include soybeans and garlic; they have a rich, full flavor, fiery but complex. They are used in cooking rather than as a table condiment.

Chili oil

Tabasco

Sambal oelek

Chilies

Sambal rudjak

Indonesian *sambals*
are spicy or hot relishes
which are usually served with food. Chilies
occur in all of them, but the degree of heat
varies according to the balance of other
ingredients. Vivid red *sambal oelek* contains only
salt, brown sugar and chilies; *sambal rudjak* has
trassi (p. 23) and palm sugar; *sambal trassi*
which is red-brown, has *trassi* added, and
sambal kemiri has candlenuts. *Sambal badjak* is a
more complex blend with garlic, shallots, *trassi*,
candlenuts and coconut milk. *Sambals* store well
in the refrigerator.

Recipes

All the recipes are for 4 but some may serve more

*T*APENADE

This olive and anchovy paste from Provence is excellent with hard-boiled eggs, sliced tomatoes or simply spread on toast. This version comes from *La Cuisinière Provençale* by J.-B. Reboul, published in 1899.

12 oz/375 g black olives, stoned
3 oz/75 g anchovy fillets
3 oz/75 g tuna in brine
1 teaspoon mustard
6 oz/175 g capers
up to ³/₄ cup/200 ml olive oil
a pinch of allspice or quatre épices
black pepper
2–3 tablespoons cognac

Blend the olives, fish, mustard and capers to a coarse paste in a food processor or with a pestle and mortar. With the motor running, pour in the oil in a steady stream, as if making mayonnaise, until you have a smooth, thick paste.
Season with the spice and plenty of pepper and stir in the cognac. Keep the tapenade in small jars, with a covering of olive oil. It can be stored in the refrigerator for several days.

ROMAN BEAN SOUP

1 lb/500 g white or cannellini beans
1 bay leaf
4 tablespoons olive oil
2 oz/50 g pancetta or salt pork,
chopped finely
1 large onion, chopped finely
1 carrot, chopped finely
2 celery stalks, chopped finely
3 large tomatoes, peeled and chopped
$\frac{1}{4}$ teaspoon crumbled sage
salt and pepper
a pinch of cayenne
2 tablespoons chopped parsley

Soak the beans overnight. Put them in a large pan, cover with fresh water, add the bay leaf, cover and bring to the boil. Lower the heat and simmer for about 45 minutes.

Heat half the oil in a heavy pan and add the pancetta, onion, carrot and celery. Cook gently until they are soft, but don't let them brown. Now add the tomato and sage and season with salt, pepper and cayenne. Cover and simmer for 10 minutes. Stir the vegetable mixture into the beans and simmer until the beans are tender, about $1\frac{1}{2}$ hours. Add the parsley 10 minutes before the soup is ready. If it is too thick, add a little more hot water. Serve with a teaspoon of olive oil over the top of each bowl.

CHINESE HOT AND SOUR SOUP

A light but warming soup from northern China.

4 dried or 4 oz/125 g fresh shiitake
mushrooms
4 cups/900 ml chicken stock
4 oz/125 g lean pork or chicken
breast, cut in slivers
3 oz/75 g bean curd, diced
3 oz/75 g bamboo shoots, cut in
slivers
2 cloves garlic, chopped
1 tablespoon light soy sauce
1 tablespoon chili oil
3 tablespoons rice vinegar
2 tablespoons dry sherry
salt
a good pinch of Szechuan pepper
2 tablespoons corn flour
1 egg, beaten
2 teaspoons sesame oil
2 scallions, sliced finely

Soak the dried mushrooms in warm water for 30 minutes, then drain, reserving the liquid. Slice the mushrooms and discard the stalks and hard centers. Fresh mushrooms can just be sliced. Pour the chicken stock into a large pan and strain in the mushroom liquid. Put in the mushrooms, meat, bean curd, bamboo shoots, garlic and soy sauce and simmer for 15 minutes. Stir in the chili oil, vinegar and sherry, and season with salt and the pepper. Blend the corn flour with 3 tablespoons water. Bring the soup to the boil and remove from the heat. Stir in the corn flour paste to thicken it. Pour in the egg through the tines of a fork, then stir it in so that it sets in light strands. Add the sesame oil and scallion and serve.

RÉMOULADE SAUCE

Pound *2 hard boiled egg yolks* with
1 raw egg yolk, 1 teaspoon mustard
powder, *½ teaspoon Tabasco*,
1 tablespoon Worcestershire sauce,
½ teaspoon anchovy paste and a
little *salt*. Add a little *olive oil* to
form a smooth paste, then beat
in up to ³/₄ cup/175 ml more, as if
making mayonnaise. Stir in
2 tablespoons wine vinegar when
the rémoulade is thick.
If you wish, add any of the
following: a few *capers, chopped
gherkin, scallion* or *parsley.*
Serve with cold prawns or
lobster or crab.

ANCHOVY CREAM

"Whip up *a gill [¹/₄ pint/150 ml]* of
cream and add to it *a tablespoonful
of anchovy essence, a teaspoonful of
made mustard* and *a pinch of
paprika pepper.* When sufficiently
whipped, put the cream into a
sauceboat, and serve with grilled
or boiled fish such as *salmon*,
turbot or soles."
The Book of Sauces, C. Hermann
Senn, 1915

SPICED EGGPLANT

4 long eggplants
½ lb/250 g onions, sliced
2 tablespoons grapeseed oil
1*½ tablespoons sesame seeds*
1 tablespoon sugar
1 teaspoon ground cinnamon
½ teaspoon ground cumin
salt and pepper
½ cup/125 ml wine vinegar
2 tablespoons water
1 tablespoon sesame oil

Put the eggplant in a large pan,
cover with lightly salted water
and cook for 12–15 minutes.
Drain and cut into quarters
lengthways. Pat dry with
kitchen paper and put the
eggplant in a serving dish.
Fry the onions in the grapeseed
oil until they are well browned.
Blend the sesame seeds, sugar,
spices, salt, vinegar and water to
make a sauce. Pour the sauce
over the eggplant, top with the
onions and sprinkle with sesame
oil. Serve at room temperature.

CARROTS WITH BALSAMIC VINEGAR

1 lb/500 g carrots
1½ tablespoons/25 g butter
⅔ cup/150 ml water
salt and pepper
2 tablespoons balsamic vinegar

Cut the carrots into thin fingers. Heat the butter, add the carrots and water, season with salt and pepper and simmer, covered, for 5–6 minutes, until the carrots are barely tender. Remove the lid, turn up the heat and let the cooking liquid reduce to a tablespoon or so. Add the balsamic vinegar, stir well to coat the carrots and serve.

BROCCOLI WITH OYSTER SAUCE

1 lb/500 g broccoli
1 tablespoon sunflower oil
2 cloves garlic, crushed
2 tablespoons oyster sauce
salt and pepper

Cut the broccoli into florets and the stalks into thick slices, peeling them if the skin is tough. Blanch for 1 minute in boiling salted water, then drain thoroughly. Heat a big frying pan or wok, then heat the oil and toss the garlic in it. Put in the broccoli and stir-fry for 3–4 minutes. Add the oyster sauce, season and fry for a minute or so longer, then serve.

SPINACH WITH SESAME AND MISO

2 lb/1 kg spinach
4 tablespoons sesame seeds
2 tablespoons dark soy sauce
3 oz/75 g miso
1 tablespoon sugar
1 tablespoon rice wine or sherry

Remove any coarse stalks from the spinach, and cook the leaves just in the water that clings to them after washing. When all the spinach has wilted, drain well and rinse in cold water. Drain again and cut into ribbons.

Toast the sesame seeds in a dry frying pan until golden. Shake it continuously or they will burn. Grind the toasted seeds in a processor or with a pestle and mortar, then add the soy, miso, sugar and rice wine. Toss the spinach with the dressing and serve at room temperature.

MUSHROOMS PRESERVED IN OIL

These mushrooms are good as part of a vegetable hors d'œuvre or for snacks and picnics, but it is only worth preserving very fresh small mushrooms.

Wipe the caps and trim the stalks of *1 lb/500 g mushrooms*. Put them in a pan with *2 cups/450 ml white wine or cider vinegar* and *2 teaspoons salt*. Bring slowly to the boil. Simmer for 3–4 minutes, then drain the mushrooms and leave to cool. Put them into preserving jars, with a few *peppercorns* and a couple of *bay leaves* in each, and fill the jars with *olive oil* to cover the mushrooms completely. The mushrooms will keep for a few weeks, and when they are finished the oil can be used for salads or for cooking.

A SALAD OF SUGAR PEAS, MUSHROOMS AND NUTS

12 oz/375 g sugar snap peas
12 oz/375 g mushrooms
2 oz/50 g hazelnuts
3 tablespoons hazelnut oil
2 tablespoons olive oil
3 tablespoons wine vinegar
salt and pepper

Trim the peas and blanch in boiling water for 3–4 minutes. Drain and rinse in cold water. Slice the mushrooms. Toast the hazelnuts in a warm oven for a few minutes, then rub off their skins in a cloth and chop coarsely. Make a dressing with the oils, vinegar, salt and pepper. Toss all the salad ingredients together, dress and serve.

Variation
Use walnuts and walnut oil instead of hazelnuts; there is no need to toast the nuts first.

TURKEY AND AVOCADO SALAD

radicchio
8 oz/250 g cooked turkey, sliced
1 large avocado, pitted and sliced
2 tablespoons pomegranate seeds
(optional)
1 tablespoon olive oil
3 tablespoons hazelnut oil
2 tablespoons sherry vinegar
salt and pepper

Tear 8–10 radicchio leaves into manageable pieces. Arrange them in a shallow bowl and put the turkey, avocado and pomegranate seeds on them. Make a dressing with the oils, vinegar and seasoning and spoon it over the salad.

Rudjak

An Indonesian fruit and
vegetable salad with a hot
dressing. The ingredients can be
changed according to what is
available.

4 oz/125 g French beans
½ cucumber
2 carrots
1 ugli fruit or pomelo
½ small pineapple
1 papaya
1 tart apple
1 slice trassi
1 tablespoon sambal oelek or
2 red chilies
2 tablespoons brown sugar
1 tablespoon fish sauce
1 tablespoon lemon juice

Cook the beans until barely
tender in boiling water. Drain
and rinse with cold water. Cut
the cucumber and carrots into
thin sticks. Break the ugli fruit
into segments, cube the flesh of
the pineapple, papaya and apple.
Combine everything in a
serving bowl.

Wrap the trassi in foil and grill
or heat it in a moderate oven for
a few minutes. If using chilies,
remove the seeds and chop the
flesh. Blend together the trassi,
sambal or chilies, sugar, fish
sauce and lemon juice, adding a
little water if necessary. Toss the
salad in the dressing and serve.

HOT-SOUR PRAWN SALAD

1 lb/500 g medium or large prawns,
shelled
3 tablespoons lime or lemon juice
2 tablespoons fish sauce
1/2 teaspoon chili powder
2 cloves garlic, chopped finely
1 stalk lemon grass, chopped finely
3 scallions, chopped finely
2 tablespoons chopped coriander
mint leaves
watercress

Dress the prawns with the lime
juice, fish sauce, chili powder
and garlic. Add the lemon grass,
scallion and coriander, and toss.
Top with a few mint leaves and
serve on a bed of watercress.

SCALLOPS WITH FRENCH BEANS

1 lb/500 g scallops
12 oz/375 g French beans
2 shallots, finely chopped
a small piece of ginger, finely
chopped
6 tablespoons rice wine or sherry
4 tablespoons walnut oil
1 tablespoon black vinegar
salt and pepper

Cut the scallops in half. Cook
the beans in lightly salted boiling
water until just tender. Drain
and rinse in cold water, then put
them in a serving dish.
Put the shallots and ginger in a
pan with the rice wine. Bring to
the boil, then lower the heat and
stew the scallops gently for 1–2
minutes, until they are opaque.
Lift them out, and arrange on
top of the beans.
Add the walnut oil and vinegar
to the pan, season lightly and
whisk together. Strain over the
beans and scallops and serve.

STEAMED GREY MULLET WITH BLACK BEAN SAUCE

1 grey mullet of about 3 lb/1.5 kg,
cleaned
2 scallions
2 slices ginger
2 tablespoons fermented black beans
1 tablespoon sherry
1 tablespoon peanut oil
a small piece of ginger, chopped
finely
1 clove garlic, chopped finely
1¹/4 cups/300 ml fish stock
1 tablespoon oyster sauce
1 tablespoon light soy sauce
1 teaspoon sugar
1 tablespoon corn flour

Make 2 deep cuts diagonally
across the body of the fish on
each side. Put the scallions and
ginger slices in the cavity. Place
the fish on a piece of foil and put
it in a steamer. Steam for about
20–25 minutes, then remove the
skin and vegetables, and transfer
the fish to a warm serving dish.

Meanwhile make the sauce.
Crush the beans lightly and mix
with the sherry. Heat the oil and
fry the chopped ginger and
garlic very briefly, then stir in
the beans and fry a few seconds
more. Add the stock, oyster
sauce, soy sauce and sugar.
Bring to the boil. Mix the corn
flour with 2 tablespoons water
and stir into the sauce. Remove
the pan from the heat when the
sauce starts to thicken and taste
for seasoning; the beans are
salty, so it may not need more.
Pour over the fish and serve.

SEA BASS BAKED IN SALT

You can bake any whole fish in a salt crust. It must be gutted and the scales and head left on. The fish will be succulent and full of flavor because the salt acts as insulation.

Choose *a bass weighing about 3 lb/1.5 kg*. Take an ovenproof dish, in which it just fits, and put in a good layer of *coarse salt* (table salt is no good for this dish). Place the fish on it and pack more salt around it and over it to cover to a depth of about 1 in/2.5 cm. Bake in a hot oven, 425°F/220°C, for 35 minutes; for a bigger fish allow about 12 minutes per lb/500 g. Break the salt crust, the skin will come away easily, and serve with a mayonnaise to which you have added fresh chopped herbs, or with rémoulade sauce (see recipe, p. 29).

SALMON EN ESCABECHE

This method of lightly pickling and
preserving fish is common in Spain,
and the conquistadores took
the dish with them to Mexico
and the Caribbean islands.

1 lemon
4 salmon fillets or steaks
salt and pepper
flour
4 tablespoons sunflower oil
1 onion, sliced
2 bay leaves
1 teaspoon crumbled oregano
1/2 teaspoon paprika
1/4 teaspoon ground allspice
1 chili (optional)
1/2 teaspoon sugar
3/4 cup/175 ml wine vinegar
4 tablespoons water

Squeeze lemon juice over the
salmon, season and leave for 15
minutes. Dust with flour and fry
gently on both sides until lightly
browned. Transfer to a dish.
Fry the onion in the oil
remaining in the pan until soft,
then stir in the herbs, spices and
sugar. Add the vinegar and
water, let it bubble for a minute,
then pour it over the fish.
Refrigerate the salmon for 24
hours before serving.

MARINATED MONKFISH

2 lb/1 kg monkfish, cubed
2/3 cup/150 ml wine vinegar
6 tablespoons olive oil
1 small onion, sliced
2 bay leaves
1 teaspoon salt
*1 teaspoon mustard seeds, lightly
crushed*
*1 teaspoon peppercorns, lightly
crushed*

Put the monkfish in a bowl. Mix
together all the other ingredients
and bring to the boil. Pour over
the monkfish and leave for up to
12 hours in the refrigerator.
Lift out the fish and fry the
pieces in oil or put on skewers
and grill for about 15~20
minutes.

BANG BANG CHICKEN

4 chicken breasts
4 oz/125 g bean sprouts
2 carrots
1 cucumber
2 scallions
2 tablespoons sesame paste
1 tablespoon sesame oil
2 tablespoons soy sauce
1 teaspoon hoisin sauce
1 teaspoon chili oil
2 teaspoons sugar
juice of 1/2 lemon
5–6 tablespoons chicken stock or
water

Steam the chicken breasts until cooked, about 8–10 minutes, then leave to cool. Cut the carrots in thin strips; peel the cucumber, cut in half lengthways and remove the seeds, then slice thinly. Chop the scallions finely.

Mix together the sesame paste and oil, the soy and hoisin sauces, the chili oil and sugar – the easiest way to do this is in a blender or processor. Dilute the sauce with the lemon juice and chicken stock until it is smooth and not too thick.

Remove the skin from the chicken, shred the meat and pile it on a serving dish. Combine all the vegetables, including the bean sprouts, arrange them around the chicken, trickle the sauce over everything and serve.

TWO MARINADES FOR PORK CHOPS OR STEAKS

I

1 teaspoon ground pepper
1 tablespoon chopped coriander
3 cloves garlic, crushed
1 tablespoon fish sauce
3 tablespoons light soy sauce

Blend all the ingredients in a processor or with a pestle and mortar. Spoon onto the meat and leave for 1 hour or more.

II

1/2 teaspoon ground pepper
2 shallots, chopped finely
2 tablespoons light soy sauce
2 tablespoons peanut oil
4 tablespoons balsamic vinegar

Whisk all the ingredients together and spoon over the meat. Leave for 1 hour or more. Grill or barbecue the chops or steaks, or cook in a medium hot oven.

FRUIT VINEGARS

Raspberries, peaches and oranges all make good flavored vinegars. Lightly crush soft fruits, chop larger ones (if using oranges include some of the peel) and put them in a large jar or non-metallic bowl. Pour over enough red or white wine vinegar to cover the fruit, put plastic wrap over the container and leave at room temperature for 2–3 days. Bring to the boil, remove from the heat and strain into bottles.

BLACKBERRY VINEGAR

A cooling and refreshing drink in hot weather.

"Put *a quart of blackberries* into a deep jar, and pour over them *a quart of white wine vinegar*. Leave them for 24 hours, then strain, and add *another quart of berries*, putting the old ones on one side. Leave for another day and night, again strain, and the third time put back the last lot of berries and the first ones, and leave again for 24 hours. Then strain through muslin, and add *one pound of sugar* for each pint of juice. Boil for 30 minutes, and when cold, bottle. This improves with age."
Summer Drinks and Winter Cordials, Mrs C. F. Leyel, 1925

INDEX

ACKNOWLEDGMENTS

The publishers
would like to thank
the following:

· TYPESETTING ·
TRADESPOOLS LTD
FROME

PHOTOGRAPHIC
ASSISTANCE ·
JONATHAN BUCKLEY

JACKET
· PHOTOGRAPHY ·
DAVE KING

· ILLUSTRATOR ·
JANE THOMSON

· REPRODUCTION ·
COLOURSCAN
SINGAPORE

MARIA JOSE SEVILLA AND FOODS FROM SPAIN
THE ITALIAN TRADE CENTRE

ROSIE FORD FOR ADDITIONAL HELP